WORDSONGS —Too Blue

BY

C. STEVEN BLUE

The Wordsongs Series

Book 2

WORDSONGS
—*Too Blue*

ISBN 0-9635499-6-0
ISBN13 978-0-9635499-6-9

Editor:
C. Steven Blue

Copy Editor:
Katharine Valentino

Proofreaders:
Paulette Schreiner
Jeremy Lee Cook

Cover & book design by C. Steven Blue

Published by:

➤ ARROWCLOUD ➤
PRESS

For more information go to www.wordsongs.com

Album Contents:

Dedication...

For anyone who feels the blues, sings the blues,
lives the blues.

For everyone who can relate to the blues in life,
this book is for you.

...Quotation...

Blue quotations from three of my favorite people:

Janis Joplin:
Don't compromise yourself. You are all you've got.

Van Morrison:
You have to understand a bit about the poetry of the blues
to know where the references are coming from.

Ringo Starr:
Got to pay your dues if you wanna sing the blues
And you know it don't come easy

...Introduction...

WORDSONGS—*Too Blue*, the second album in The Wordsongs Series, is all about the blues: hardships and heartaches, failed relationships, the trials and tribulations of love throughout the years—paying the dues to sing the blues. Personal and evocative, C. Steven Blue presents another set of revealing and inspirational wordsongs.

The Wordsongs Series

Each book in this series contains 20 pieces designed to be similar in scope to a music record album, with side one and side two, but instead of songs it is made up of a style of poems called wordsongs. Each book is a concept album, with a general theme running through it, told in verse format.

Wordsongs are the original creation of C. Steven Blue, who also created a definition for this concept:

word'song, n. [AS. wordsong.]
  1. a poem that is like a song or could be a song
  2. verses that tell a story in song-like rhythm, often with a refrain
  3. a song that you read

...Inspiration

. . . If music speaks, do words sing?

Some music speaks to your senses without words.
Wordsongs sing to your senses without music.
Wordsongs speak to your inner rhythms.

The 20 wordsongs in this album tell a story.
Any music that they sing to you . . .
must come from the inner ear of your own imagination;
the musical tapestry of your mind.

Turn the pages and listen . . .
to these words.

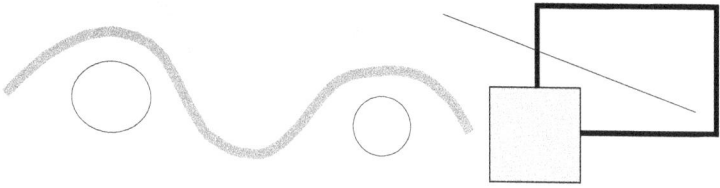

Side One . . .

Blue Rose Suffering

All the false promises you gave
All the rivers you were gonna save
All the children lying in their graves
Can't hear you any more

All the love you can't return
All the lessons you'll never learn
Until your tattered world
Comes crashing down on you

How many dreams
From so many dreamers
Wither up and die
Can you tell where they went
When you no longer see
The sparkle in Love Song's eyes

I was the eternal smile
You've stolen it away
You've robbed and pulled and pricked me
Till I'm full of your decay

Blue rose is suffering
Sing it gospel style
Famous spirits now join in
You walk a familiar mile

First love returns to you
And spreads her fertile wings

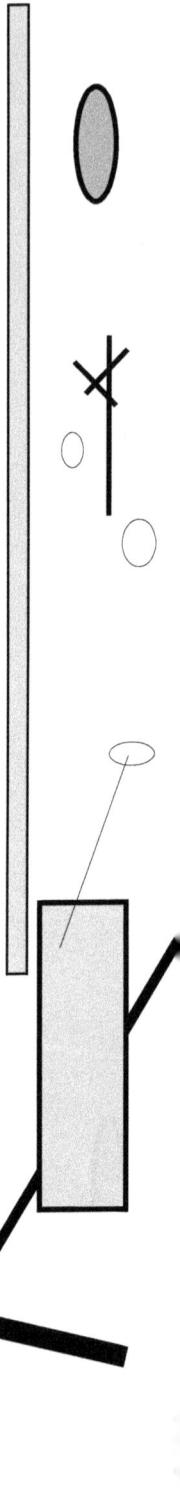

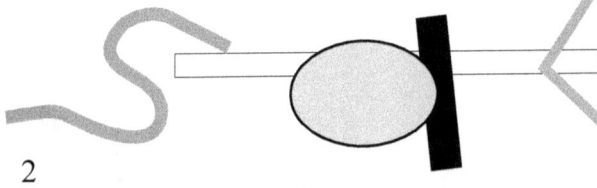

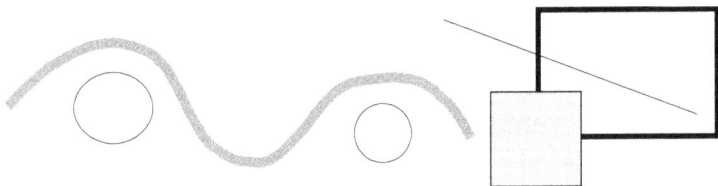

You find old friends
Sing old songs
And think of long gone things

I used to be a gentle soul
But your world has crushed me
I gave you all my faith and trust
But you still don't trust me

I went to school
To learn your golden rule
But you do unto others
However you please

I loved a girl
I gave her my heart
But her commitment
Was only a tease

Blue rose suffering
Sing it gospel style
Famous spirits now join in
As you walk the familiar mile

First love returns to you
And spreads her fertile wings
You find old friends
Sing more old songs
And think of long gone things

How long you go on suffering
To heed the muse's call
When all you need is time, you think
To get up when you fall

To write—and write—and write—and write
And write some more again
If only you had the time
        To write
You know the muse would send

You know they say
If you live long enough
You'll disprove all your beliefs
Not only the ideas
And principles you stand for
But all of the metaphors
Causing all of your grief

And all of what's matter
In the universe
Be it light or be it dark
        Means nothing
In your little scheme of things
Except the inspiration
That gives you the spark
        And the time to write it
        And to dream . . .

Blue rose is suffering
Sing it gospel style
Famous spirits now join in
You walk a familiar mile

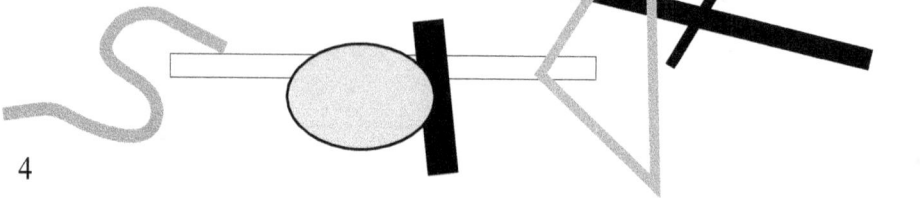

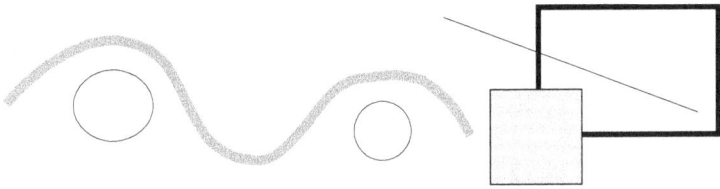

First love returns to you
And spreads her fertile wings
You find old friends
Sing old songs
And think of long gone things

All You've Got

They say life is for living
Whatever you choose
But you've got to eke out
An existence

Unless you are born
Of the privileged few
You always will meet
With resistance

They say love is for giving
Without thought of reward
Well you've got to surrender
        To win

Unless you realize
You're not in control
You know you have yet
To begin

And don't give up
It may not sound like a lot
But don't give up
Your dreams are all you've got

And some day
You're gonna break right through
All the good you've done
Will come back to you

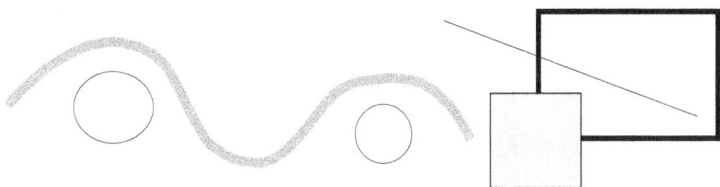

Time flies by
When you're trying to live your dreams
There's never enough time
          It seems

And every obstacle
Tries to get in your way
While you're trying to make it
To a better day

Don't give up
It may not sound like a lot
But don't give up
Your dreams are all you've got

And some day
You're gonna break right through
All the good you've done
Will come back to you

Life Is Like A River

Life is like a river
That's been tearin' thru the ground
Sometimes it moves so quickly
You can't know where it's bound

And then . . . sometimes . . . it's very still
It doesn't make a sound
But woman . . . when I need you so
You never are around

I have so much I need to do
This straight life leaves no time
I'm sick of playing games
'Cause now I've barely got a dime

I need someone (who'll bide her time by my side)
To help me stand up strong
A woman who will stick by me
Even when she thinks I'm wrong

      I've gone so far
      I've lost so much
      Now this warm heart
      Just needs your gentle touch

Life is all around you
Every day you prove it true
But until you see your life alone
Life will remain something new

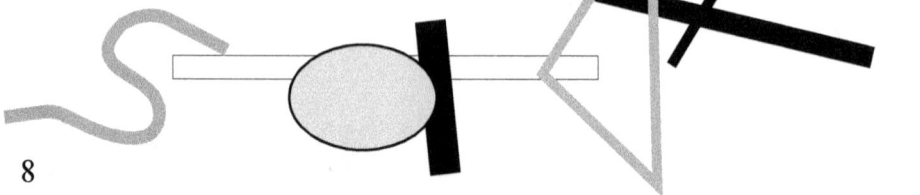

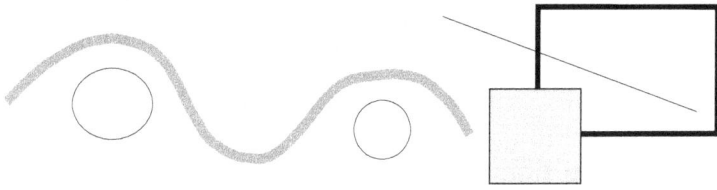

So if you ever think you're lonely
And you need some company
If you want someone who really cares
Then come and stand by me

    I've gone so far
    I've lost so much
    And now this gentle heart
    Just needs your warm touch

'69 Theory Unsure

The soft brightening stars
Were calling my name
Return to the ocean
From whence sprang Life's game

They kept right on calling
Till I finally knew
That I must go down now
Or forever be blue

Got the blues in my body
The blues in my soul
They're quicker than lightning
And hotter than coal

If you don't come back darlin'
You know that I'm crying
'Cause you said you don't want me
I feel like I'm dying

Baby . . . baby . . . baby
If you could see me now
You'd know me
Oh baby . . . baby
If you wanted to
You'd show me

But baby . . . oh baby
You're gone

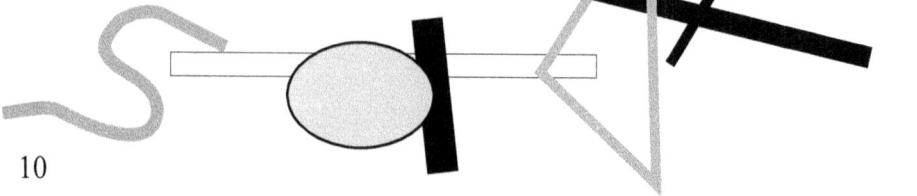

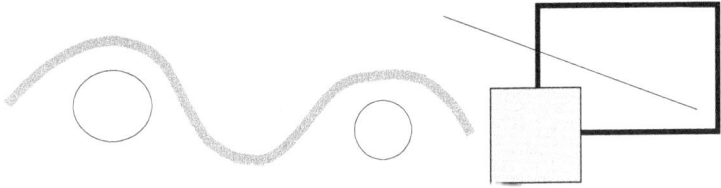

Bye baby . . . bye baby
Bye-bye

Then some friends on the sand
Helped me realize
The reality of the situation
They could sympathize

I am a part of all of it
It's a part of me
It is what has been
It is what will be

You know we all can see ourselves
Although sometimes we're scared
The journey you're on will help your soul
To show how much you've cared

If I could direct you my Love
I'm sure you would know
These ocean sky dreams
And the love you could show

It's the '69 theory
. . . Unsure
Just one more day with you
        My love
And maybe we would
Find the cure

11

Baby . . . baby . . . baby
If you could see me now
You'd know me
Oh baby . . . baby
If you wanted to
You'd show me

But baby . . . oh baby
You're gone
Bye baby . . . bye baby
Bye-bye

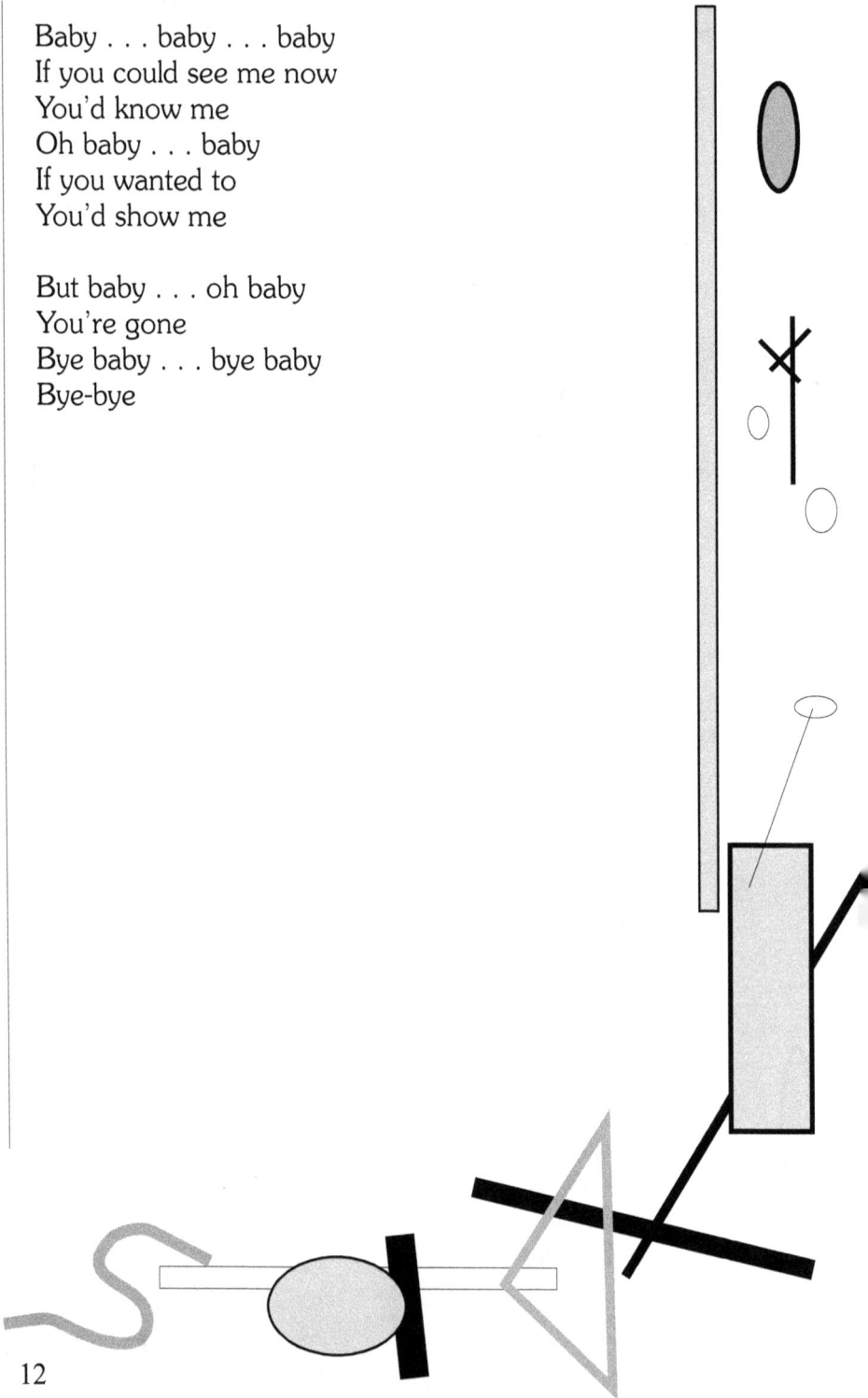

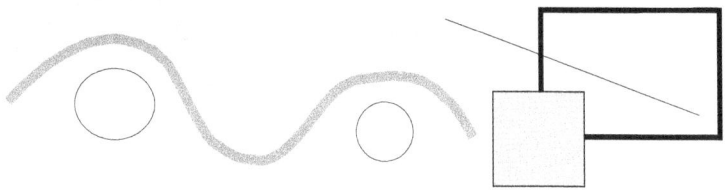

Green Trees

The world
        God
    Ourselves
Our experience
—Everything about us

As if you cared
Green trees for me
Blue skies cry
I wonder why
As if you cared

Just for once
To shine with the sun
Just for the reaction
A fraction of satisfaction

Just for once
A new life begun
Just to be true
A small clue—what to do

As if you cared
Green trees for me
Blue skies cry
I wonder why
As if you cared

Just for a dance
That has begun
Just for the pairing
The awareness of sharing

Just for a chance
Not to run
Just for the daring
The chance to get your bearing

As if you cared
Green trees for me
Blue skies cry
I wonder why
As if you cared

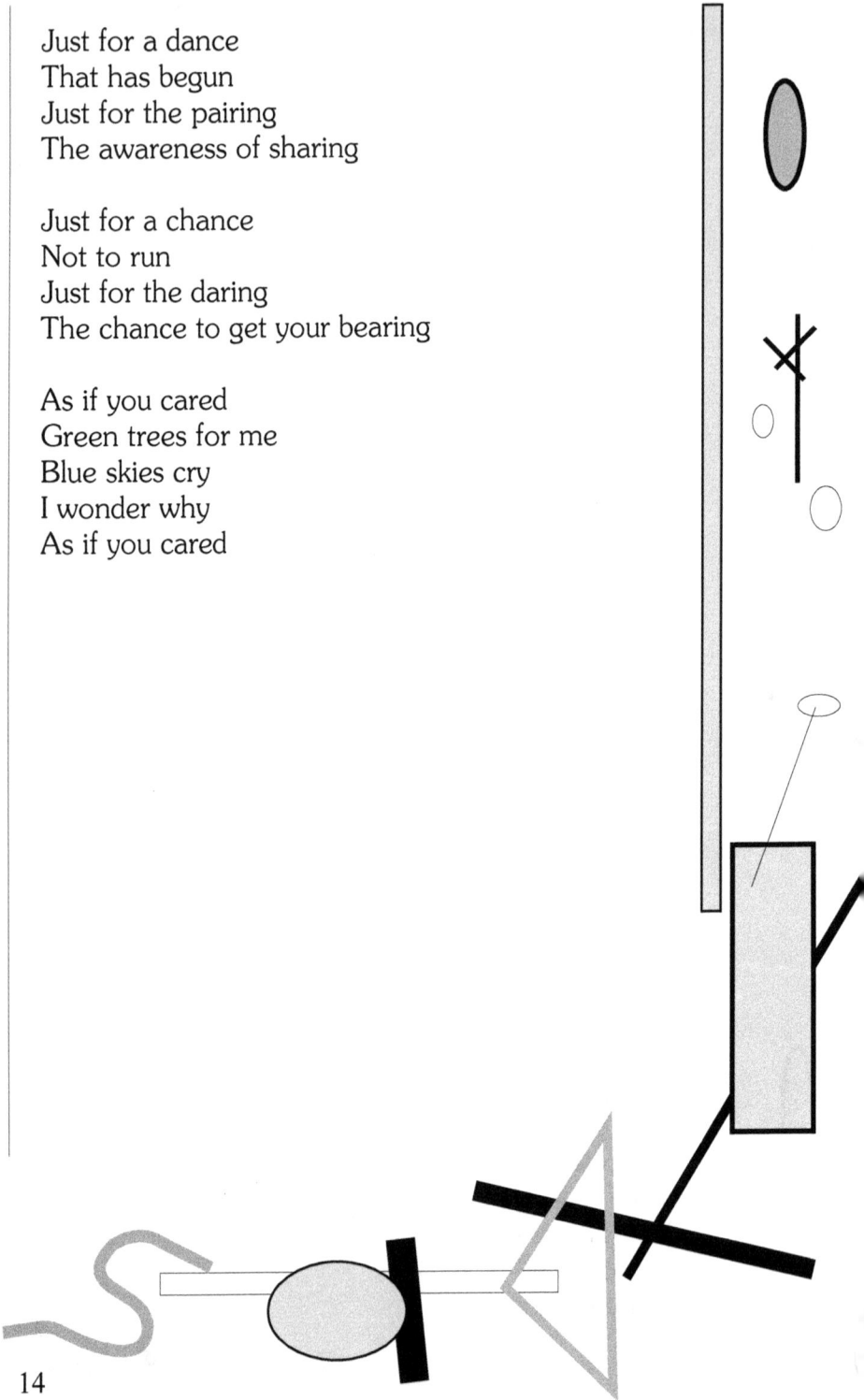

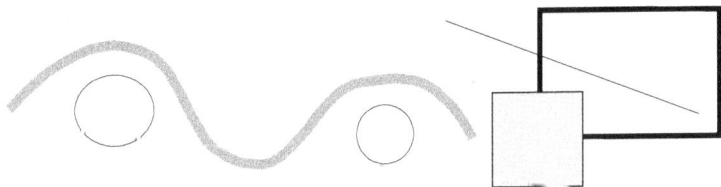

Wake Up To My Tears

Woke up from a long sleep
Two days very ill
My body still aches
From the bad food I ate

My bones ache too
From so much rest
Many dreams passed through . . .
I think as I get dressed

In my dream I knew the way home
It was a treacherous journey
I have been there before
I hoped that you would join me

I really wanted to share it with you
If you just would have been willing
But instead . . .
I only woke up to my tears

Cold . . . like my life
Grey . . . like my life
I never really get there
You're always out of reach

Broken . . . like my life
Lonely . . . like my life
You're always there in my dreams
But I only wake up to my tears

15

I work all day
Clean up, pay the bills
I pay my own way
. . . I paid yours too

In my little spare time
I try to work on my dreams
But they always end up shattered
By the outside greedy matters

And you don't want to know
What you can't really see
Or maybe you're just scared
Of what it actually could be
. . . If the dreams
Became the reality

In my dreams . . .
I know the way home
I always think you'll follow
You said that you would love me
Until always and tomorrow

But you never stick around
I turn around and you are gone
And I just wake up alone again
To my tears

Cold . . . like my life
Grey . . . like my life
I never really get there
You're always out of reach

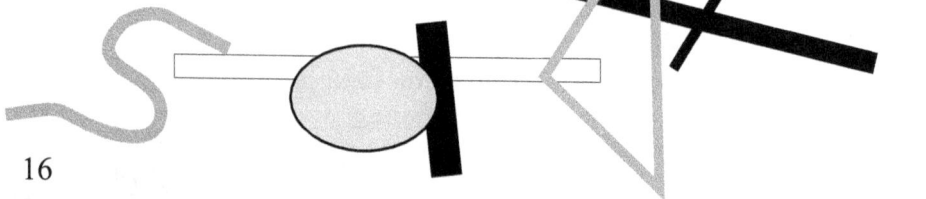

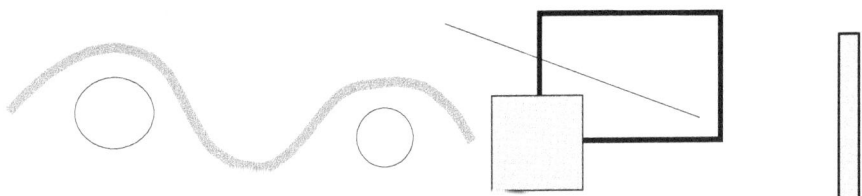

Broken . . . like my life
Lonely . . . like my life
You're always there in my dreams
But I only wake up to my tears

The time goes by so fast
Things just keep piling up
Just enough time to get it done
Not enough to work on the dreams
          That are mine

I've always had to work and slave
For other peoples' dreams . . . I pay
The obstacles never let me save
          For that rainy day
          I only find when I dream

Cold . . . like my life
Grey . . . like my life
I never really get there
You're always out of reach

Broken . . . like my life
Lonely . . . like my life
You're always there in my dreams
But I only wake up to my tears

17

Tempted By An Angel

You did the best you could do
Worked hard to make things right
But no matter how hard you try
Some things just don't work out in this life

You paved the road to the Garden of Eden
You even made her your wife
But in the end she left you
With nothing but guilt for the strife

Tempted by an angel
Speaking words of love
Tempted by an angel
A vision from up above

Tempted by an angel
She was speaking the words of love
Tempted by an angel
Is all you were guilty of

You can't ever seem to find someone
Willing to commit like you do
Yet you've still got your children
And your dreams
To carry you through

But you still see that sparkle
That shines in her eyes
You still remember it all

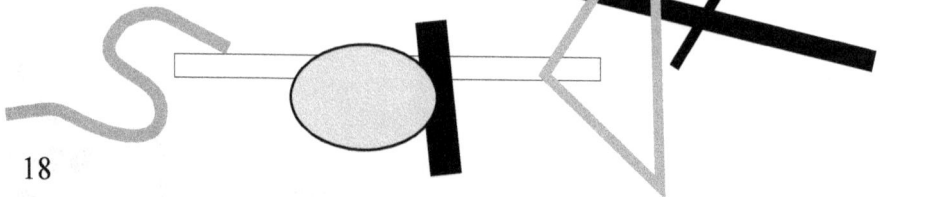

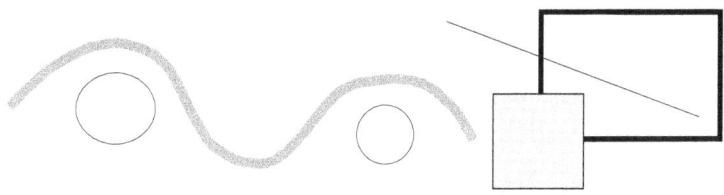

And no matter how you try to ignore it
. . . Sometimes
You still hear the angel's call

Tempted by an angel
Speaking words of love
Tempted by an angel
A vision from up above

Tempted by an angel
She was speaking the words of love
Tempted by an angel
Is all you were guilty of

Dreamer & The Schemer

He had something to say
She didn't want to listen
He had moral fibre
She had itchy fingers

Eventually you see
Deep down inside you know
The dreamers and the schemers
Come and go

She was caught up in her own world
They were two young people in love
But she was caught up in a world
He had to let go of

Someday you'll remember
What you learned in your youth
Eventually you have to stop and listen
To learn the truth

Love so strong
What went wrong
Dreamer and the schemer
Where have you gone
        Carry on
Dreamer and the schemer

Drowning in your sorrow
Love let go so fast

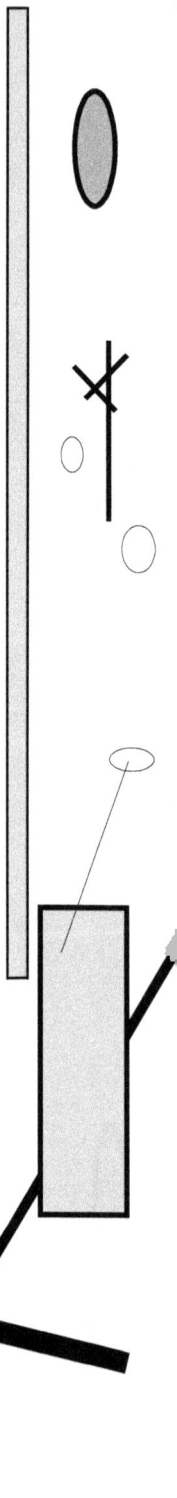

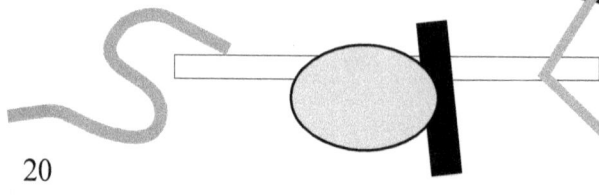

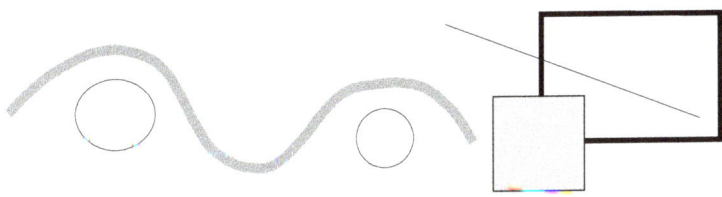

Nothing for tomorrow
Now that love won't last

There are two sides to every story
Two sides to every tale
There are those who feel the glory
There are those who just set sail

There are two sides there to look at
You're blind if you don't see
There's your side . . . yes
—But seriously
There's also me

He had something to say
She didn't want to listen
He had moral fibre
She had itchy fingers

Eventually you see
Deep down inside you know
The dreamers and the schemers
Come and go

Love so strong
What went wrong
Dreamer and the schemer
Where have you gone
        Carry on
Dreamer and the schemer

Go It Alone

When I was young
I was very naive
I gave my faith so easily

Trusted everyone
Who came into my circle
I thought they all wanted to help me

I'm grown up now
And not as gullible
But I've been alone inside for so long

Still I would like to
Reach out and trust
Someone with my song

It's a long . . . long road
When you go it alone
But what other choice do I have

Because every time
I reach out and trust
You stab me in the back

I sit in this same cubicle
Year after year
Writing and struggling to be free

From the material chains
That bind me
To this spiritually bankrupt reality

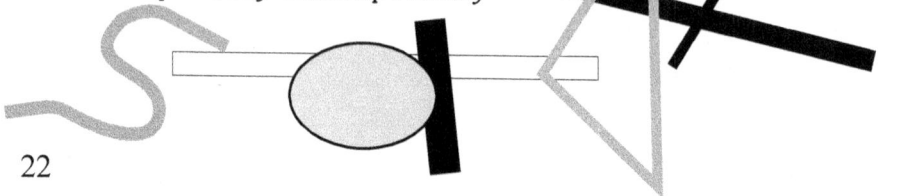

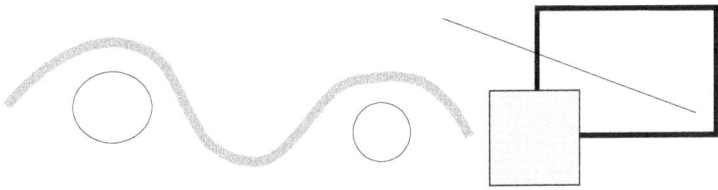

Can you show me what is real
Can you show me how to feel
Right now

Can I sing it
Can you hear me when I bring it
Or do you know how

It's a long . . . long road
When you go it alone
But what other choice do I have

Because every time
I reach out and trust
You stab me again in the back

I'm just a lost soul
Living in a world I can't control
Looking for someone
To make me feel whole again
       Seems you just can't win

. . . So I go it alone

It's a long . . . long road
When you go it alone
But what other choice do I have

Every time
I reach out and trust
You stab me in the back

23

Time To Cut Loose

Just sittin' here
Watchin' time go by
Waitin' for the call
So much to do
To get out of here
This time you know I won't fall

Yes, bad luck has come
And bad luck has gone
And bad luck has come again
But this time . . .
When I get out of here
You know I'm gonna win

Waitin' for my job
Waitin' to move
It's time to cut loose

      'Cause it's the lovin' I've seen
      The lovin' I've known
      And it's growin'
      A new day is comin'
      It's been on the rise so long
      And it's showin'

Just sittin' here
Watchin' time go by
Rememberin' me and you

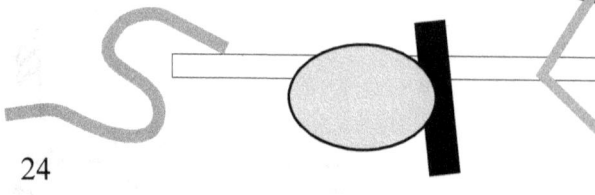

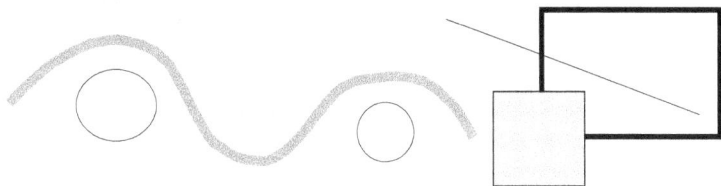

The plans we made
The dreams we had
This time they're gonna come true

Yes, good luck has come
And good luck has gone
And good luck has come again
But this time . . .
When I get next to you
You know we're gonna win

Rememberin' you
Rememberin' my youth
It's time to cut loose

> 'Cause it's the lovin' I've seen
> The lovin' I've known
> And it's growin'
> A new day is comin'
> It's been on the rise so long
> And it's showin'

Waitin' for my job
Waitin' to move
It's time to cut loose

Rememberin' you
Rememberin' my youth
It's time to cut loose

25

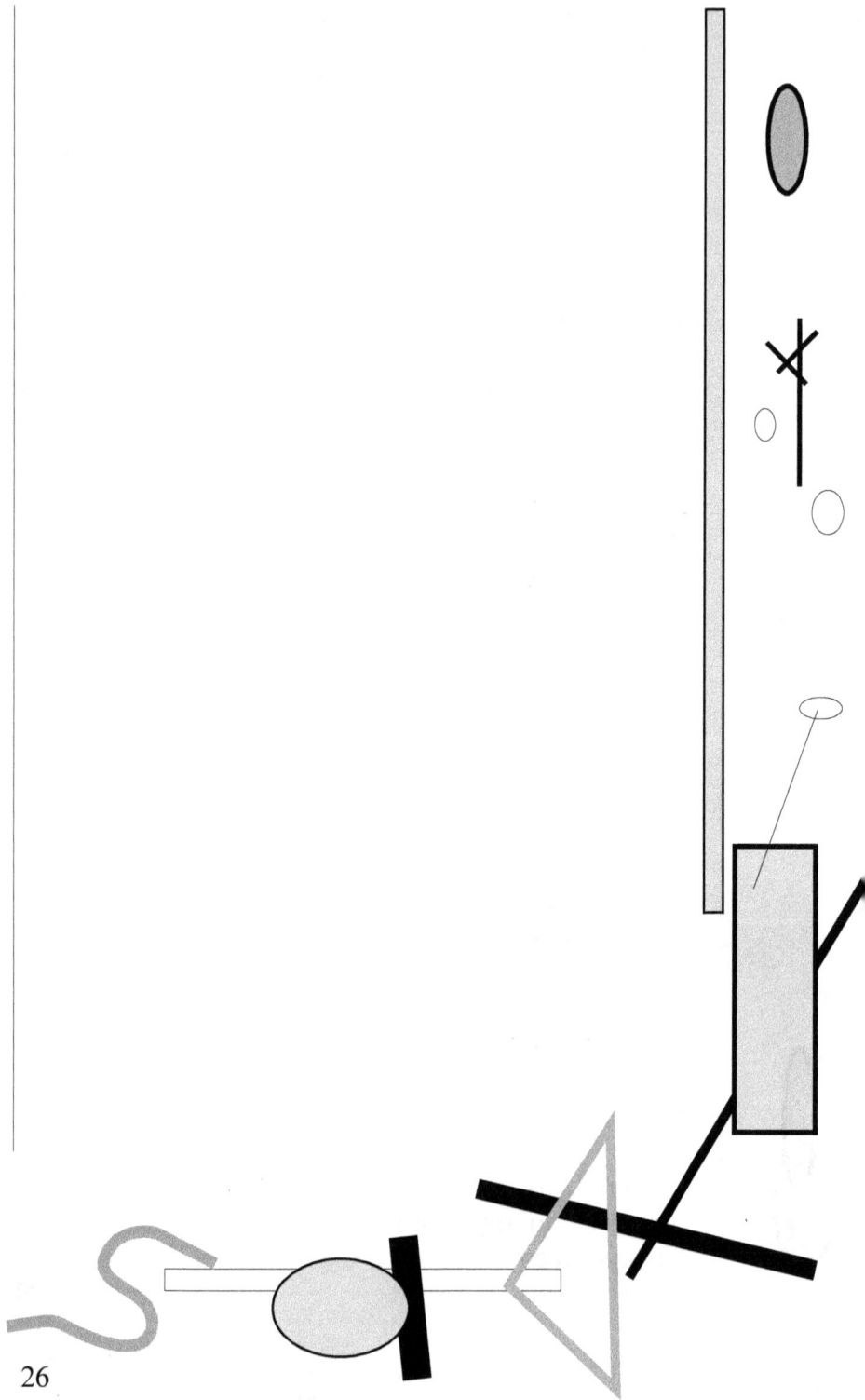

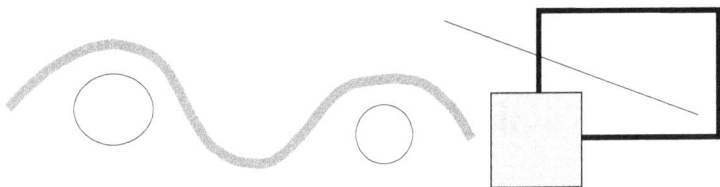

Side Two . . .

From Thee—
Out Of Control Zone

Scraping the sand off the bottom
following tracks long forgotten
footsteps erased from time
miracles in the distance
—a very steep climb
it's time to light the perspective view
of the endless new

Because you've followed the dreams
through the years
seen the highs, the lows
and the tears
overcome the fears
and the magic soothes your troubled soul
but where is thee—control

The waves know it
for they calm when I sing
the sun knows it
for it shines when I bring it to you

Why lose your grasp
of the true path
don't get caught in the net
don't forget 7th heaven

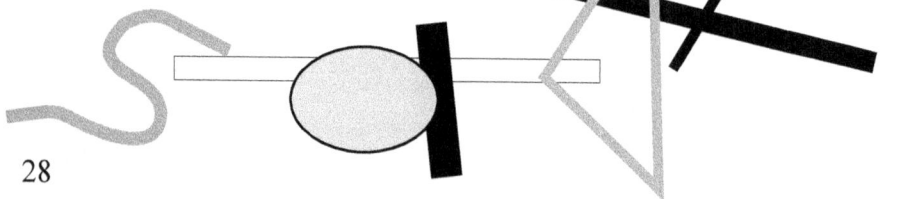

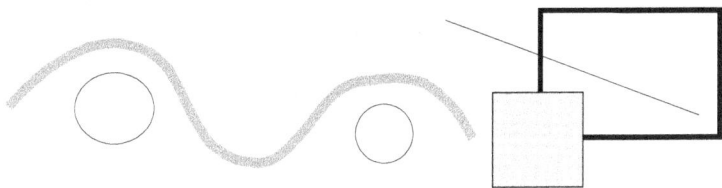

there are so many bumps
on this cross-track blues road
. . . a note of notion
by the heartbreaking ocean

Musical sparks made us aware
a sign of the times was in the air
so patch it up
like the seams in your jeans
remember the magic
we had in our teens
the magic that soothes your troubled soul
oh, where is thee—control

Don't ever forget
the dreamers and the schemers
the seedy greeters
        greed to the max
no pacts or parcels full of caring
for the sharing of your soul
oh, where is thee—control

Times so rare and friends so few
where has it gone
and what has it gotten you
what time is it, Miracle Swing
what time is this thing you bring
—the magic
that soothes your troubled soul
oh, where is thee—control

Why do I dwell on this dogma
causes caused
and cautioned by the wind
the business grin begins again
is the sparkle burnt to the crisp
in the wisp of time
did you forget how to shine

Save it for the savior
save it for the sun
can you be wild and still be true
is it still inside of you
the anonymous enemy
pays the dues for your blues
show him what is real again
and believe you can still
see your dreams

For the schemer always schemes
and the dreamer always dreams
and the magic . . .
soothes your troubled soul
oh, where is thee—control

The waves know it
for they calm when I sing
the sun knows it
for it shines when I bring it to you

Oh, the magic of your touch
seems so much
          seems I knew you
          seems I knew you

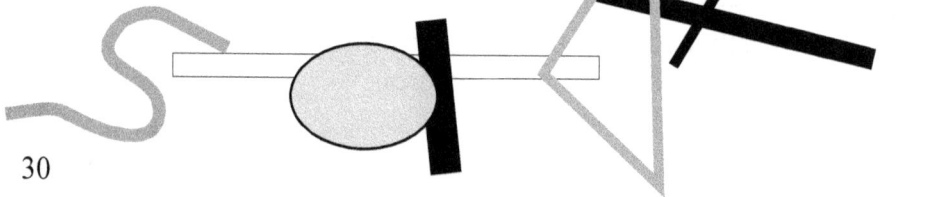

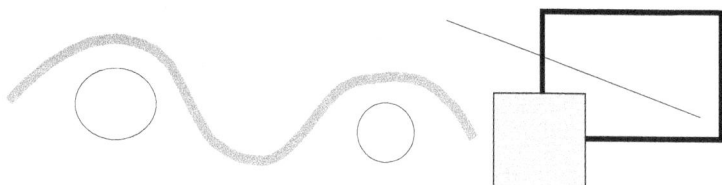

The indefinable nature
of the true magic we found
will always be inside me
it is always there, unbound
I will never forget you
though your manic ways took their toll
and the magic soothes your troubled soul
but where is thee—control

31

Born Out Of Time

Born out of time
Without a chance to shine
Spending all my time
Just trying to make a dime

In and out of love
And then alone again
Something from above
And then it's gone again

It seems like I was born
For emotional pain
Every time I warm up to you
You push me away again

I guess I was just born
                To misery
I just don't understand
It must be my destiny

Born out of time
Without a chance to shine
Spending all your time
Just trying to make a dime

Born out of time
But you can change your mind
Take the time to find
And you will shine

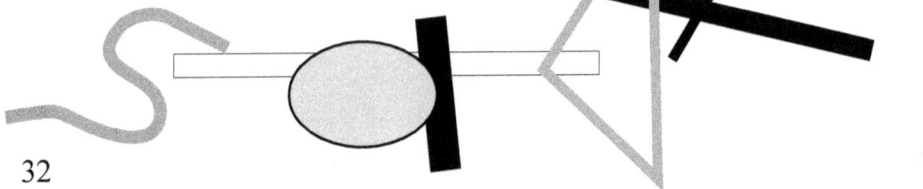

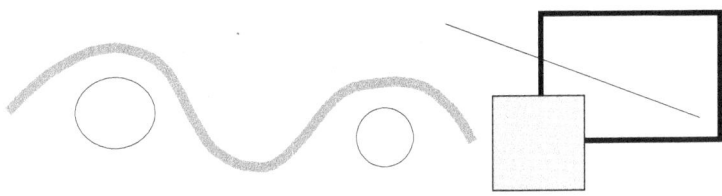

Give me the reason
To be alive
I've always been a survivor
Give me the will to survive
Not just a nine-to-fiver

It's you . . . down in the meadow
Dancing in the grove
Surrounding purple flowers
The honey smoking clove

Today is the future
The journey has begun
You and I together
Walking in the sun

Something more will come of this
Because we're in our prime
You and I will be the ones
We will shine this time.

Born out of time
Without a chance to shine
Spending all your time
Just trying to make a dime

Born out of time
But you can change your mind
Take the time to find
And you will shine

33

Blue

Blue . . . as can be
Desire cannot be filled
hungry for your love
So far away

Blue . . . tell my heart
To try and settle down
Tell it to remember
Love won't stray

Blue . . . since you've gone
And left me stranded here
Moping through the night
In cloudy skies

Blue . . . on my own
TV is no company
For the blurry teardrops
In my eyes

Blue . . . blue
Can't get away from you
You're the colour of my mood all day

Blue . . . blue
No matter what I do
Always seems just like you're here to stay

—When my baby goes away

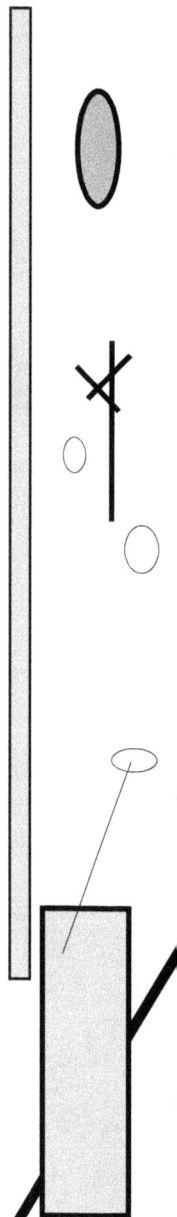

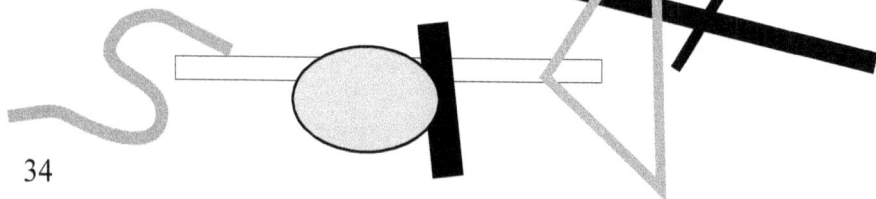

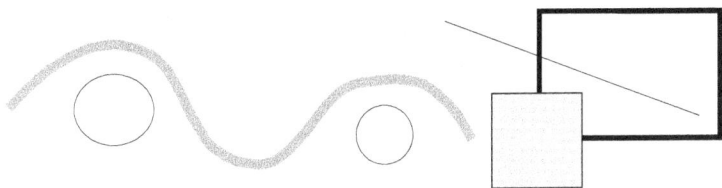

Blue . . . how I sigh
In the morning—quiet time
Finds my mind still drifting
Off to you

Blue . . . standing still
Don't know which way to move
Trying to find some way
To renew

Blue . . . it's just the way
So long without you near
Can't get you off my mind
No matter what

Blue . . . it's just not right
The darkness is my home
Gathers like a gloom
Down in my gut

Blue . . . blue
Can't get away from you
You're the colour of my mood all day

Blue . . . blue
No matter what I do
Always seems just like you're here to stay

—When my baby goes away

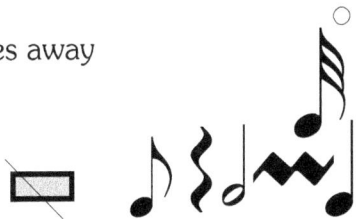

35

A Love Incomplete

You say you love me
. . . oh so much.
You want to experience
my every touch
that I might have to give,
that you might get to feel.

Yet you want to discover
what more might be out there;
to uncover and feel
all the world has to offer.

Your young lust is longing—
your body aches to describe
what another young lover
might have deep inside.

How can I decide
to keep or let you go?
How can I live with
what I might have to know?

How can I taste
your kisses, so sweet,
that will leave me so stale
with a love incomplete?

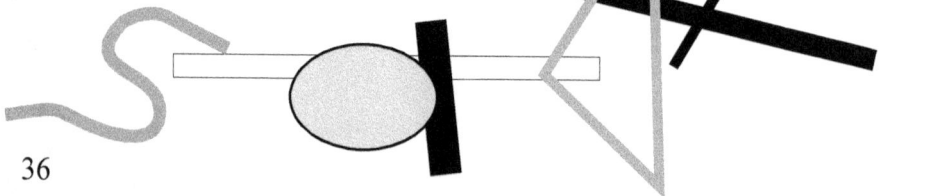

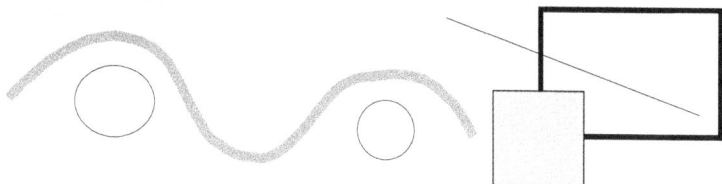

Sweet and tempting,
Your words stick in my throat
like a stale, powdered doughnut
—yesterday's.

I want you, I need to . . .
feel all that you have,
yet the catch strikes so deep!
Don't you know?

How can I keep you . . . but let you go?
My world isn't ready
for a relationship like this.
Or is it just . . . I cannot stand
the thought of you with another man,

as I burn for your kisses
and long for your touch;
afraid I might lose you
—what I treasure so much.

How can I decide
to keep or let you go?
How can I live with
what I might have to know?

How can I taste
your hunger, so sweet,
that will leave me so stale
with a love incomplete?

37

Find Yourself

It's hard sometimes
letting you go.
I was looking for a full-time love,
you know;
and you were looking
to find yourself.

But it's always fun
watching you grow.
Observing self-discovery
makes my insides glow.
Does it show?

So go on flower,
. . . bloom!
I'll just dance
around my room
and tingle inside
for the knowing.
Go on flower,
bloom.

It's awkward sometimes
when you call
and I have nothing
to say at all
because I know
you're just looking
to find yourself.

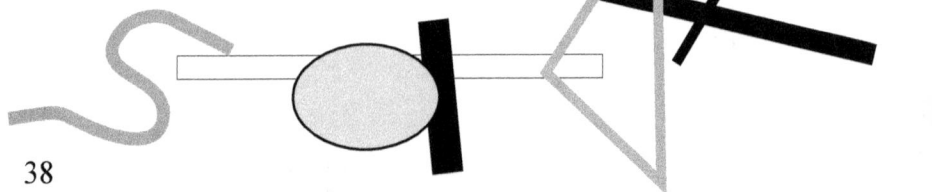

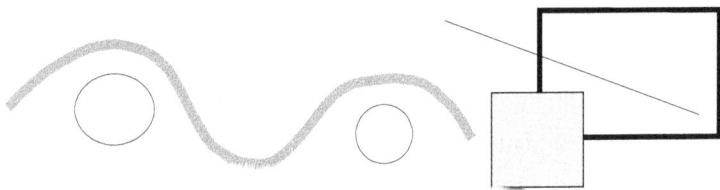

There's so much
I'd really like
        to say,
but it all stems
from yesterday.
So I let it go
and watch you
looking to find yourself.

So go on flower,
. . . bloom!
I'll just dance
around my room
and tingle inside
for the knowing.
Go on flower,
bloom.

Afterglow

It's so hard . . . don't you know
I love you so
But I just can't stay here anymore
We've gone through this pain
So many times
But this time the wounds are just too sore

I'm so tired . . . I'm so weary
It's just no good
Why can't we just say . . . I love you
And let go like we should

Come on . . .
Share another sunset with me
Just one more sunset
Before we go
After all . . .
It's the way we started
Now it could be our afterglow

We've grown a lot . . . together
That's what love is for
They say
But like we said in the beginning
If we grow apart
Then it must be okay

Because growth is what matters
You know things always change
I wanted to grow . . . with you
But it's not mine to arrange

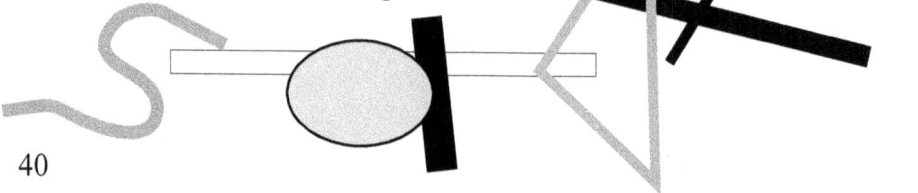

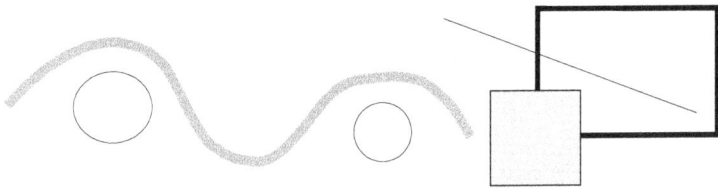

So come . . .
Share another sunset with me
Just one more sunset
Before we go
After all . . .
It's the way we started
Now it could be our afterglow

If we've outgrown our welcome
Let's just leave it . . . and say
That we parted as we started
True friends . . . growing our own way

I need to get on with my own life now
And look beyond troubled times
We've both got a lot to share . . . somewhere
But I need a love that truly rhymes

In my heart I've already left
You pushed me away long ago
I keep on hoping
Something will change
But it just rearranges

So come . . .
Share another sunset with me
Just one more sunset
Before we go
After all
It's the way we started
Now it could be our afterglow

41

Just Like A Dog

They say don't kick a dog
When it's down
But I been kicked
All over town
Up one side and down the other
Till it makes no sense to bother
Even gettin' up off the floor
          No more
Just kick me again
And I'll roll right out the door

And just like a dog
There ain't nothin' I can say

So I'll just howl—let me be
And I'll just howl—set me free
I'll just howl—let me go
All I can do is howl—don't kick me no mo'

They say you gotta have compassion
And concern for your brother
Be kind and loving
Help one another
But no matter how I try
You keep kickin' my back
You've got a big ego
Humility is what you lack
Now you kick me once more
And I roll right out the door

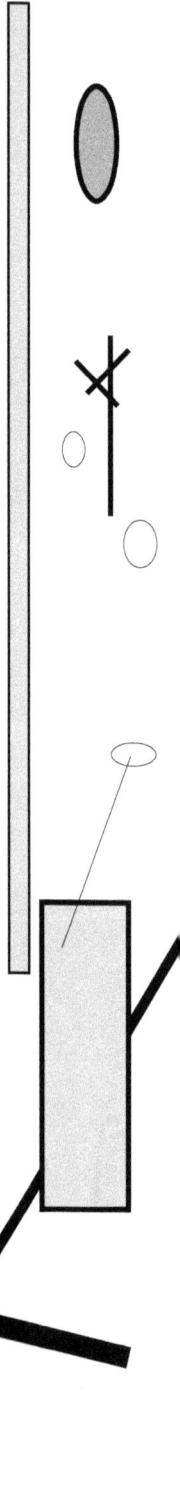

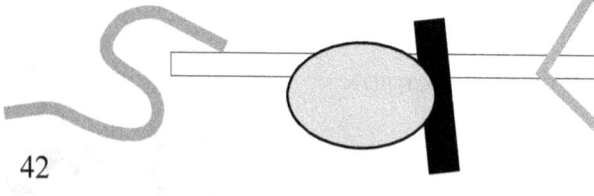

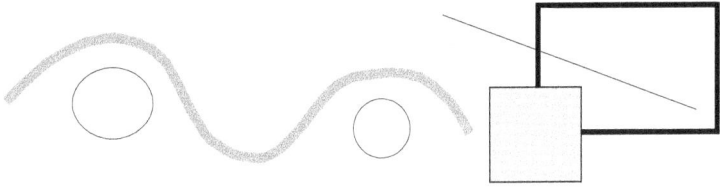

And just like a dog
There ain't nothin' I can say

So I'll just howl—let me be
And I'll just howl—set me free
I'll just howl—let me go
All I can do is howl—don't kick me no mo'

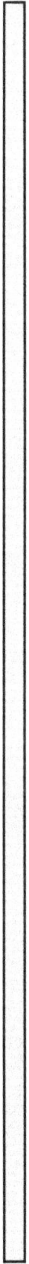

You had quality products
But now they're gone
Only profit motivation
Keeps you carryin' on
People are just
Another commodity
They don't matter much
In this hypocrisy
You just keep kickin' 'em
And watch 'em roll right out the door

And what's it matter anyway
Just like a dog
There ain't nothin' I can say

So I'll just howl—let me be
And I'll just howl—set me free
I'll just howl—let me go
All I can do is howl—don't kick me no mo'

43

Rock It In The Socket

Hey—
Superstition man
Layin' your line on my woman
But don't try to lay it
On me—man

'Cause I've seen that plan
Before
   Hidin' around
     Behind my door
   Sneakin' around
Behind my back
Waitin' for me to go out
Then fillin' my woman with doubt

Hey—
Rock it in the socket
Before you walk out my door
Honey . . .
Rock it in the socket
Like you never did before

Rock it in the socket
Wake up . . . baby . . . take me
Rock it in the socket
Earthquake woman . . . shake me

—Once more

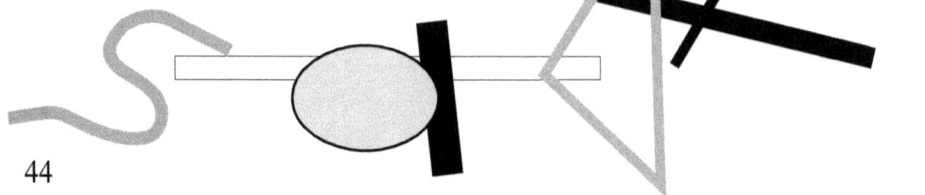

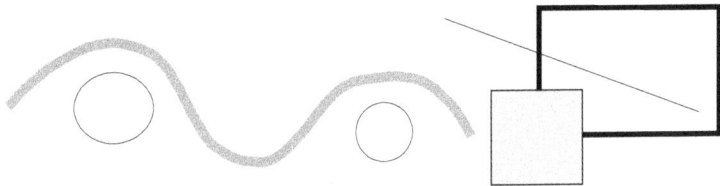

Hey—
Superstition man
Takin' it while you can
But the only way you can get it
Is by sneakin' in on another man

Listen to me . . . woman
Don't you fall under his spell
'Cause superstition's gonna get ya
You know damned well

So rock it in the socket
Before you walk out my door
Honey . . .
Rock it in the socket
Like you never did before

Rock it in the socket
Wake up . . . baby . . . take me
Rock it in the socket
Earthquake woman . . . shake me

—Once more

Where are you
My native sky
  Where are you
    My hunger
  Do you ever wonder
Why I linger
Just waiting for the mingling
Of love

45

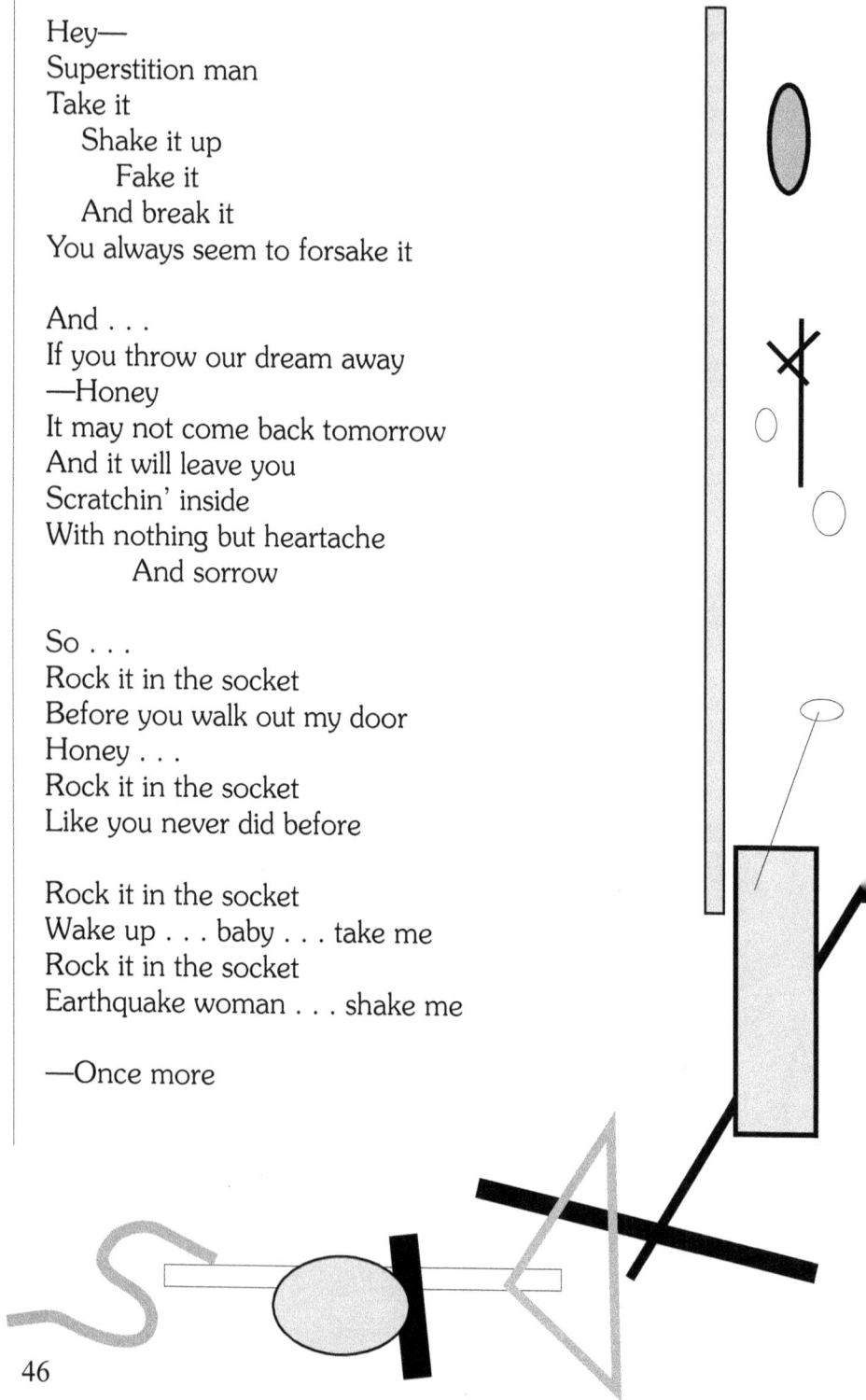

Hey—
Superstition man
Take it
    Shake it up
        Fake it
    And break it
You always seem to forsake it

And . . .
If you throw our dream away
—Honey
It may not come back tomorrow
And it will leave you
Scratchin' inside
With nothing but heartache
        And sorrow

So . . .
Rock it in the socket
Before you walk out my door
Honey . . .
Rock it in the socket
Like you never did before

Rock it in the socket
Wake up . . . baby . . . take me
Rock it in the socket
Earthquake woman . . . shake me

—Once more

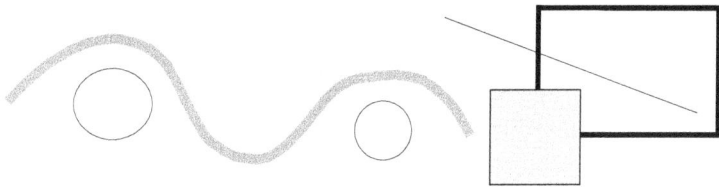

Bat's Ass Blues

I never had a real mentor
I had to fight my way
Through this dark ol' jungle
On my own

I did have a hero though
Old sweet Winston
But he died and left me here
All alone

Then you came along
And gave me some solace
—Some sweet love
And clear reprieve

But every time I got too close
That black cloud would come creepin'
—Hit me hard
And you'd just up and leave

You'd act like I was your man
Love me hard and fast
Then play aloof
Like I didn't know the score

Then you'd swoop down again
From your dark and danky perch
To bite me in the ass
Once more

47

I got the bat's ass blues
On the porcupine highway
Might as well be
On the highway to hell

'Cause I fell off the barstool
When you rode off in the night
And left me hangin' high
At the River Ridge Hotel

Got the bat's ass blues
You know I paid my dues
To come down from your spell
Oh well!

Got the bat's ass blues
From my head down to my shoes
You bit me
And it all went to hell

Drivin' along
The Snake River Canyon
Just to hear some bangin'
On those 88's

I only came to help you
A friend in need
Screamin' down the highway
Through those western states

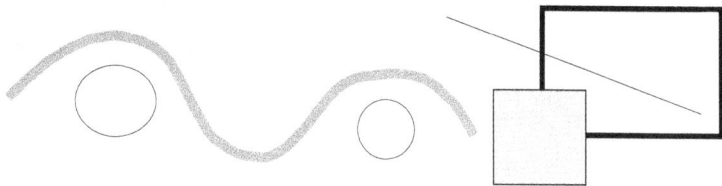

We all were on your side
But you didn't want to hear it
You said you would be true
But you coughed it up again

Just another excuse
For your hot and sultry lust
That left me—just crumbled
In the end

You said you were gonna stop
Yer awful cheatin' ways
That always left you hollow
And sore

But the road is always callin' you
Just wanna move on
Leave me suckin' the blues
Once more

I got the bat's ass blues
On the porcupine highway
Might as well be
On the highway to hell

'Cause I fell off the barstool
When you rode off in the night
And left me hangin' high
At the River Ridge Hotel

49

Got the bat's ass blues
You know I paid my dues
To come down from your spell
Oh well!

Got the bat's ass blues
From my head down to my shoes
You bit me
And it all went to hell

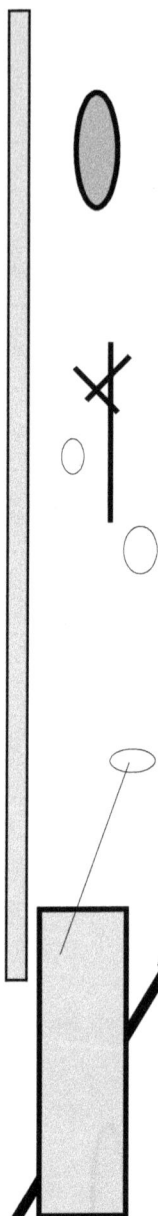

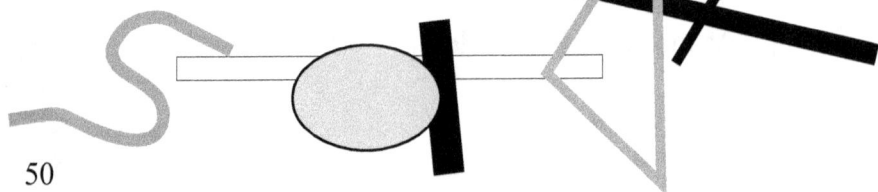

Said you didn't wanna hurt me
Didn't wanna do no harm
You just wanna feel secure
Safe and warm

The good times are so rare
Only here for a brief moment
Then the bad things creep back in
—Like a storm

Got the bat's ass blues
You know I paid my dues
To come down from your spell
Oh well!

Got the bat's ass blues
From my head down to my shoes
You bit me
And it all went to hell

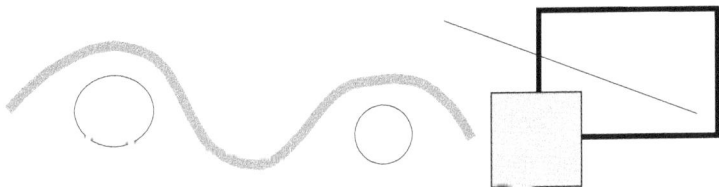

Are All My Love Songs Written?

I saw it in your eyes once
Not so long ago
I felt it when you smiled at me
With that old familiar glow

But the magic seems so rare now
In the autumn of my years
The things that used to tingle inside
Can now bring me to tears

Oh, the long and cloudy years
The range of which ran broad
Dissolve into the aches and pains
That now make me feel flawed

I've slipped . . . and fallen down
Don't know if I can get back up
To feel again, what I felt back then
When you filled my loving cup

Are all my love songs written?
Is this the last hurrah
Will I never again be smitten
By the beauty that I saw

51

Are all my love songs written?
Did it all just end too soon
Will I ever again . . . feel the passion
Or the howling of the moon

I felt it in the way you moved
In the once again so new
The moon was full, your curves were round
Oh, how your fancy flew

But the flying is less frequent
And the motivation's mild
The things that used to drive me mad
No longer are so wild

I've settled into the distance
And hung my tears to dry
Now all I have . . . is a vague resistance
To call my dreams and try

Are all my love songs written?
Is this the last hurrah
Will I never again be smitten
By the beauty that I saw

Are all my love songs written?
How could it all just end so soon
Will I ever again . . . feel the passion
Or the howling of the moon

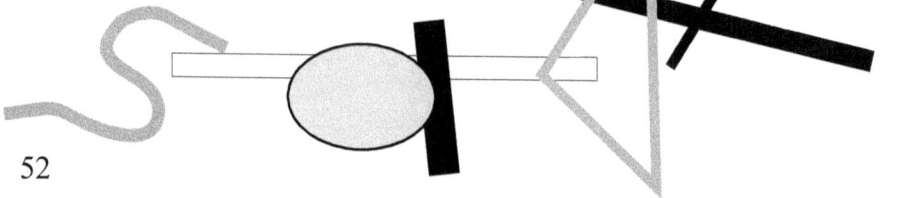

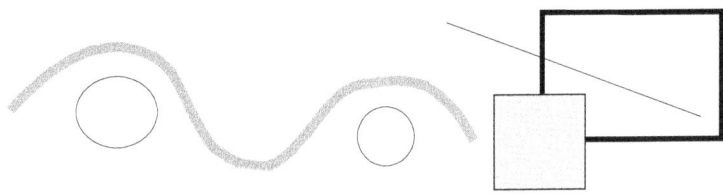

The small and whispered wonders
That barely recall my youth
The forget-me-nots . . . that I forgot
In all the tangled truth

It's a melancholy madness
        That I've stumbled
It now creates this sadness
        And I'm crumbled

In a lifetime of Love's passion'd memories
And heartfelt, often missed discoveries
I truly do admit
        that I am humbled

Are all my love songs written?
Is this the last hurrah
Will I never again be smitten
By the beauty that I saw

Are all my love songs written?
Did it all just end too soon
Will I ever again . . . feel the passion
Or the howling of the moon

Index of original composition dates

About The Author

Throughout his life, poet C. Steven Blue has experimented with music and songwriting. As a result, many of his poems are songlike. Steven has collected these poems into this series of books called *Wordsongs*; each book containing 20 poems and resembling a record album in scope and concept. We hope you have enjoyed the second *Wordsongs* album and will continue to read this unique series.

C. Steven Blue grew up in Los Angeles, California. Poetry has poured out of him since he was a boy. He won his first poetry award at age 12. However he did not start to write seriously until he was 18. That was in 1968. The tumultuous events of the 1960s were exploding all around him, inspiring him to write with greater fervor and frequency.

After various jobs in his youth, Steven began a career in Hollywood stage production that lasted 27 years. He is now retired and living in Eugene, Oregon. He continues to write and perform his own poetry, publishes his own and other's works, and produces and hosts local poetry events.

About The Symbols

PEACE BETWEEN MAN AND WOMAN

Steven designed this symbol in 1966 (at the age of 16) as a tribute to the Hippy idealism of the 1960s.

Now a registered trademark, it is both a valid and timely symbol for the third millennium.

AQUARIUS WITH LEO RISING

Steven also designed this personal symbol in 1966 as his own signature. His natal astrological sign is Aquarius, with Leo rising, represented here by the Sun (Leo's ruler) rising over the symbol of Aquarius.

About The Artwork

All of the computer graphics, symbols, pictures and illustrations in this book were created by C. Steven Blue.
All photographs are owned by C. Steven Blue.

MORE BOOKS

BY

C. STEVEN BLUE

WILDWEED

Black Tights — Poetry X

S.O.S. ~ Songs Of Sobriety ~
A Personal Journey Of Recovery

WORDSONGS

Published by

ARROWCLOUD
PRESS

For more information go to www.wordsongs.com